I

Tolen Media books may be published for educational, business or sales promotional uses. For more information, please email tolenmedia@gmail.com.

Tolen media website: http://www.tolen.media (@tolenmedia)

Tolen Media® and the Tolen Media logo are trademarks of Tolen Media Publishing..

First Tolen Media Paperback edition published in 2020

Library of Congress Control Number: 2020916443

Tolen, Christopher C.
    She Be Sacred: 30 ways to love her more / Christopher
Conrad Tolen. ===1st Ed.
    ISBN: 979-8-61371-364-6
    1. Men---Psychology 2. Masculinity (Psychology)

SHE BE SACRED

30 Ways To Love Her More

by Christopher Conrad Tolen

Dedication

I dedicate this book to pure, unconditional LOVE, without whom this book could not have, and would not have, ever been written. Thank you for your showing me the way.

I surrender.

I choose you!

Introduction

Initially, we're going to need to agree on one absolute fact that you must innerstand before reading any further. This absolute fact is not up for debate, argument, consideration, contemplation or vulnerability to any ifs, ands or buts from anyone, anywhere, at any time or from any platform, disposition, perspective, religion, culture or creed. It is absolute truth; an ancient truth which is so absolute that the very act of saying it out loud will begin the process of what will be the beginning of your personal journey to loving your Goddess more.

This absolute fact that I'm speaking about is quite simple and you already read it in the title of this book, however, to embark on this journey properly, you MUST begin by saying it out loud.

"_____ is sacred." (Fill in the blank with the name of your significant other.)

Repeat that 7 times out loud.

Why 7? I like 7. 7 is a great number.

She be sacred. That she be. Sacred should be her middle name, but for now let's let her keep the one she was given.
Now some of you may not really innerstand just how divine she is. In fact, SHE may not even innerstand how divine she is, so let's start off with the first way to love her more which is by recognizing what in fact makes her so sacred. That way when you say "_____ is sacred.", it will be coming from a place of proper emotion and intention; therefore a place of true love.

"Ego Knows Love Not"
(a poem by Christopher C. Tolen)

To water her
Is to love her
To shine light on her
Is to love her
To shield her from danger
Is to love her
To heal her wounds
Is to love her
To adore her beauty
Is to love her
To find delight in her sweet scent
Is to love her
To sever a rose from her bush
Is ego and ego alone

CHAPTER 1: CHOOSE HER

Choosing the Goddess that you, as a God, know in your heart, soul and spirit is the one Goddess that deserves your surrender is the first step in loving her more. If you're choosing a woman who you know isn't the ONE, then you are more than likely creating a wider chasm to cross before you're able to eventually seal the deal with the ONE.

There are a fafillion factors involved when choosing a lifelong companion and the biggest mistake to make in the choosing process is to allow superficial reasoning to cloud your better judgment. Before we get into why you must choose her and make sure she always knows that you are choosing her, choosing her completely and choosing only her, we must make sure that we're choosing the ONE.

This is the part where you go deep into your heart, your mind, your psyche and ask yourself, ask your higher self, ask any deities that you trust, ask the Universe, your ancestors and any other guides or helpers you can think of, if this is the Goddess for you, and if you're the God for her. Ask to remember her.

It's up to you to listen, to feel, to contemplate, to consider, to meditate on and to ultimately decide for yourself if you will be CHOOSING this Goddess as the one you will be surrendering your whole being to and receiving surrender from. The reasons for this choice must be the right reasons, not reasons stemming from low vibration. No Goddess will be able to fully surrender to one who has not consciously chosen her completely, with all faculties available and with utter finality.

When she's right, you WILL know. There will be no itch in the back of your mind whispering, "What if?" When she's right for you, the Universe will work magic to let you know. Spirit will bring synchronicity that must be recognized, but the fact remains that it will be communicated to you by your own higher self and other "higher ups" as well. You must not let lower vibrations and material or lesser desires cloud your judgment as you're listening for the highest truth with regard to the perfect union between you and your Goddess.

If she's not right for you, and deep down you know it, walk away, lovingly and respectfully. Save yourself headaches, heartache and troublesome stress by giving the big brain more influence over your decision-making than the little brain.

If by chance you choose the wrong Goddess who is not perfectly aligned with you and for you by the stars, the Universe and all that is divine, sacred and holy, then you will have invited MISalignment into your life. You will have invited in the wrong person with whom to attempt all the things recommended in this book and your results may not be as favorable as they would be if your choosing involved your highest wisdom and intelligence.

Furthermore, if by chance you have already chosen the wrong Goddess who is not perfectly aligned with you (you'll know or may already know) then attempting the things recommended in this book may not prove beneficial as you may be surrendering your power to someone who might abuse it or not be worthy of such surrender.

One of the craziest things about life is that we've all made somebody better for somebody else. If moving on is an option, sometimes it's best to let go and let God.

If you already have a child(ren) with her and would like to remain in the relationship for the highest benefit of the child(ren) I pray you are able to find your way into a sacred connection with her that is aligned and divine nevertheless. This is not impossible. Greater miracles have occurred. May the blessings of all the heavenly hosts be upon you if this is the case.

Once the choice of choosing the correct Goddess for you is made by you, you must make your Goddess aware of your choice. Tell her that you choose her, come up with ways (different paths for different people, of course, so be creative!) to show her that you choose her, tell everyone you know that you choose her and begin the process of habitually continuing to not only choose her over and over again, but also to let her know as often as possible that she is the chosen one.

For anyone seeking more to consider when choosing a life partner I highly suggest reading "The Science of Happily Ever After: What Really Matters in the Quest for Enduring Love" by Ty Tashiro. This witty author takes you deep into the science of choosing the perfect partner for you. I can't say enough about how little any other book can help your relationship if you start off choosing the wrong life partner.

Single men, especially, who are doing the work on themselves to vibrate higher and attract a higher vibrating Goddess to your vortex should read this book and learn more about what mistakes are commonly made when choosing goes wrong and how to avoid that. This book is a gem and will save you a lot of heartache, time and money if it's read and applied. Just do it.

CHAPTER 2: RECOGNIZE THAT SHE IS A GODDESS

Your woman is divine. There are no two ways about it. She is absolutely a Goddess in every sense of the word. Whether she recognizes it herself or not is not a factor in whether or not YOU must recognize it in order to love her completely. So let's explore her divinity. Exploring that will, no doubt, require exploring your own divinity as well.

There is a term "sacred feminine" that has been around for a very long time. It has been expressed in many ways, in many languages by sages and saints the world over from time immemorial. It is partnered with and can only be truly innerstood and appreciated by its opposite and complementary which is the sacred masculine. This is who and what the highest version of you is and what you must learn to recognize in yourself in order to fully recognize and appreciate the sacred feminine in her.

History has recorded a very wise master teacher named Yashua as saying, in effect, that "ye are gods", which translates into modern English as "you are gods". Yashua was the given name of a Hebrew man known to many by various terms including, but not limited to, teacher, scholar, prophet, shaman, rabbi, messiah, christ, messenger, holy man, seer, witch, astrologer, etc, depending on what education you received regarding this man who for the sake of argument I'll refer to as the master teacher known as Jesus Christ to the majority of the modern world.

In his statement that "ye are gods", Jesus was quoting a famous scripture from the Old Testament of the Bible (I'll quote the King James version since it's the most widely-used worldwide), Psalms 82:6 which states:

"I have said, Ye are gods; and all of you are children of the Most High."

The reason Jesus was making the statement "ye are gods" in the first place happens in the 10th chapter of the Bible's Book of John beginning with verse 30 with Jesus making what was, at the time, a very bold and, to some, a very blasphemous statement denoting that he was a divine being. In Israel 2000 years ago, that statement was punishable by stoning to death. The following excerpt will show the context of his statement:

(30) I and my Father are one. (31) Then the Jews took up stones again to stone him. (32) Jesus answered them, "Many good works have I shewed you from my Father; for which of those works do ye stone me?" (33) The Jews answered him, saying, "For a good work we stone thee not; but for blasphemy; and because that thou, being a man, makest thyself God." (34) Jesus answered them, "Is it not written in your law, 'I said, Ye are gods?' (35) If he called them gods, unto whom the word of God came, and the scripture cannot be broken; (36) Say ye of him, whom the Father hath sanctified, and sent into the world, Thou blasphemest; because I said, I am the Son of God? (37) If I do not the works of my Father, believe me not. (38) But if I do, though ye believe not me, believe the works: that ye may know, and believe, that the Father is in me, and I in him." (39) Therefore they sought again to take him: but he escaped out of their hand.

Jesus said to those seeking to condemn him that, because their own scriptures stated that all humans are gods and children of the

Most High, he was in no way blaspheming by calling himself the son of the Most High. This has been interpreted by different people in different ways, but I'll leave it up to you to decide if you believe his statements meant that Jesus, you, the woman you love, myself (the author), and every single person on this Earth is in fact a child of the Most High, which would mean they are sacred, they are divine and they deserve just as much love and respect as you and everyone else, regardless of whether or not they know, believe or acknowledge their own divinity.

If you're still with me, then let's proceed. Pretty much every culture on the planet has age-old memories of humans being created by one or more divine beings or gods. If that holds true, then Jesus's notion that everyone is in fact a descendant of "God" must hold some merit. I could go on and on for hours about the various cultures that hold this notion to be true. I could also go on for hours listing the countless histories, myths, legends and scriptures that back up this claim however I will leave that for you to research on your own. I'd rather focus on the various methods which you may use to infuse more love into the treatment of your Goddess.

In the spirit of us all being holy and divine creatures, let us approach our Goddess and all things related to our view of and treatment of her from this perspective, and this perspective only. If you're having trouble seeing her from this perspective I suggest you do some research on the term "sacred feminine" and spend some time learning exactly what it means to hold something as sacred. Then come back and read this book again.

For now, in the spirit of moving through this material, suffice it to say that she (and you) are children of the MOST HIGH GOD and are sacred, holy, divine and spiritual beings made of light. That light is being interpreted as what modern science has called matter or substance. That substance is sacred. Your sacred woman IS a Goddess. Make her aware that you acknowledge that. She will feel more loved because of it and she will also be much happier knowing that you are aware of your own divinity.

CHAPTER 3: RECOGNIZE THAT YOU ARE A GOD

The next step in learning to love your Goddess more is to apply everything from chapter two to yourself. That means that "Ye are god". You are a God. You are sacred. You are divine. You are holy. You are a spiritual light being that exists on many planes and must begin the journey of discovery that will enable you to fully encompass your totality, especially as it pertains to the partnership you hold to be sacred.

Many ancient religious texts have been misinterpreted and/or mistransliterated. Some would go so far as to say even deliberately altered to remove personal power from divine individuals such as you and your Goddess and place it elsewhere outside of yourselves. I can't think of one "messiah" in history who would have considered that anything other than a blasphemy of the highest offense. They all knew, and all proclaimed the divinity of man and came to teach methods by which that divinity could be sought out, recognized, honed and utilized for humanity's highest good.

"It takes one to know one" is one of the most common retorts heard on a playground and probably because it contains so much truth in such a short phrase. It really does, though. It takes a divine being to recognize another's divinity, so if you're unable to recognize your woman as a sacred and divine Goddess then it might be that you are unable to recognize the same in yourself. Let's begin there and get some sacredness education embedded into our programming so we can THEN go back to chapter one and start over there.

I was 21 years old when the first inklings of my own divinity began to trickle into my consciousness from books that I was reading at the time. So to save time here I'm going to suggest a few books to read that aided me in learning to recognize my own sacredness, and which I'm sure will assist you in doing the same. They aren't the longest reads, so you'll be done in no time, but the concepts, and their explanations contained therein, are very powerful yet simple comprehensive tools one, especially a Westerner, might use to gain serious insights into one's own divinity and manifestation capabilities.

"The Celestine Prophecy" by James Redfield taught me about energy, synchronicity and coincidence, help from the astral plane, from your soul group and other related concepts that I'm sure will shed some light on your innerstanding of just how divine you and your Goddess are. That book is a good place to start if you're lacking the ability to see divinity in yourself or your significant other.

"Conversations With God" (parts 1, 2 and 3), a series by Neale Donald Walsh, came next for me and really gave me the words to say so many things that I felt but had no clue how to express in spoken language. Mr. Walsh is a godsend and I advise anyone seeking to ponder and innerstand more about their own divinity to read all three volumes of that series. I promise that once you start you won't be able to put it down and you might even read all three books again. Yes, they are that powerful.

Personally that series really assisted me with releasing old, outdated notions that patriarchal culture has infected us all with. Notions that are divisive and unloving must be released if one is to graduate to a level of consciousness that allows for seeing one's woman as the Goddess that she is and seeing one's self as the God that you are.

"Toltec Wisdom: The Four Agreements : A Practical Guide to Personal Freedom" by Janet Mills and Don Miguel Ruiz is the last book I will suggest for now since reading these will definitely give you a foothold on the journey. Self-discovery requires one to become more authentic and honest with one's self and mate. This will allow you to see you both as the divine beings that you are while beginning a journey towards higher consciousness in general that will in many ways afford you the ability to love your Goddess more divinely and yourself as well.

So in recognizing that you are a God, a child of the Most High, I will leave it at this, since these fine authors have all done such an immensely wonderful job that it would do no justice to anyone to make attempts to redefine the timeless wisdom they've so eloquently and so comprehensively laid down for generations to come. Just trust me that reading those books will help. They helped break me out of a low-vibrational state of patriarchal perspective that was not conducive to my treating the women in my earlier life as the Goddesses that they were. These books combined were very instrumental in the first functional relationship I ever had where I actually had a desire to be faithful, and despite the fact that it didn't work out, she and I are still friends to this day who respect each other as the God and Goddess that we are. Powerful books, I tell you.

CHAPTER 4: HELP HER TO LEARN MORE ABOUT HER SACREDNESS

After you finish each of the books listed in the last chapter, give them to your Goddess to read so that you both may share in the education of your shared divinity. This can be a personal journey, but as the saying goes..."two heads are better than one", so why not combine your efforts, learn together and use the experience as a tool to solidify the bond you're attempting to perfect.

There's a lot of sharing to be had and when you see each other breaking out of your shells and shattering your old paradigms together, your respect for each other will grow as well as your love for each other. Doing the work together is a powerful glue that works wonders towards honoring each other and building a more solid foundation for the relationship as a whole. So share those books, read them together, whatever it takes to get the information inside those books into both of your brains ASAP!

"The Celestine Prophecy" was even made into a Hollywood movie, so it might be a good idea to suggest a movie night where you watch it together. That's one way to get introduced to the information more quickly and without the need to read one more book. Alternatively, you both may want to read the book after watching the movie to get more insights into the author's wisdom. You won't be disappointed.

Along the way, you may come across other books or articles to share with each other and I recommend doing just that. The more you both educate yourselves on how divine you both are, the more your love and respect for each other will grow and the more you will be able to easily recognize the other's divinity, the more sacred that will cause your union to become. Be sacred.

CHAPTER 5: LEARN MORE
ABOUT YOUR OWN SACREDNESS

It makes zero sense to learn how sacred your Goddess is without focusing just as much time educating yourself about your own sacredness. You are a God and the degree to which you are unaware of this fact is directly proportionate to the time, effort and resources you need to dedicate towards becoming aware of just how sacred you are.

It literally does take one to know one, so if you'll ever truly appreciate your Goddess in all her majesty, you must in fact learn to appreciate yourself in all of yours. You must rise above the mundane, the low vibrational, the run-of-the-mill notions about being a man and start to learn about, embrace and emulate the godly qualities that someone calling himself a man should be exhibiting.

A deep analysis of oneself is in order at this point. This will require you to remove all distractions from your focus. Go somewhere quiet where you will be alone and undisturbed for some time while you do some serious thinking and meditating on where you've been, where you are now and where you're going, as a man who wants to be the God that you know you are.

The first step is to look over your past, especially with regard to past relationships, and ask yourself what went wrong. This will require you to be completely honest with yourself and learn to step outside of your ego and look at yourself from the perspective of "the watcher". For some this may be a simple task, but for many it may prove difficult.

If separating yourself from ego proves difficult for you or seems like a foreign concept then some help might be necessary and while I can't tell you what you must do in order to separate yourself from ego, I can outline what worked for me and let you decide for yourself if you need something as extreme as what was necessary for me. I can promise you this much, the method I chose wasn't always comfortable. It required a lot of courage and dealing with discomfort and trusting in the process of personal growth. Some like to call this "doing the work". If you're not prepared to do the work then you're reading the wrong book.

I was required to use a shamanic technology called dimethyltryptamine (or DMT) for me to, for the first time, be literally separated from my ego and shown just how ungodly I had been living up until that point in my life.

For those of you who are unaware of what DMT is, it is a neurotransmitter in the tryptamine family that is synthesized by a pinecone-shaped gland in the center of your brain called the pineal gland, known throughout history in cultures across the planet as the "third eye". While DMT is classified as a psychedelic, and illegal in some areas, keep in mind that it is already in your body right now and using it will simply be adding a bit more to allow you to reach higher states of consciousness. (I don't recommend breaking the law, but I do recommend traveling to a place where the shamanic technology is legal in order to have the safest experience possible when having a ceremony.)

DMT is the main ingredient in different shamanic technologies from indigenous peoples around the world such as the psychedelic brew Ayahuasca (prominent in and originally from the Amazon region of South America) and changa (which is a DMT-infused smoking blend, typically made from combining extracts from DMT-containing plants with a blend of different herbs and ayahuasca vine and/or leaf to create a mix that is 20–50% DMT, making what some refer to as "smokable ayahuasca").

Let me be clear, these technologies are not to be taken lightly, are not "toys" to be trifled with and can actually cause serious damage to one's psyche if not administered properly, in the correct set and setting and with the aid of a qualified guide to lead one through the experience properly. This is not for the faint of heart, but for those who seek to truly transform themselves into a higher vibrational being intent on growth and personal development.

With the proper guidance of a competent and qualified shaman, these shamanic technologies can be used to provide a quite profound experience that will allow someone whose culture and programming has denied them access to their sacredness to be shown their divinity in an unforgettable way that not many alternatives are capable of.

Now it must be stated that these, some might call extreme, shamanic technologies are not absolutely necessary for each and every human being to separate from ego, achieve enlightenment or simply better one's self, however, for the author of this book, it was necessary.

I honestly feel that coming across DMT about 14 years ago, learning to use various forms of it and doing so (extensively at first and then less so over the years as I became a shaman and "needed" it less and less) was the main catalyst for me to become a better husband, father and all-around more positive and love-based human being that is a benefit rather than a detriment to my community.

To put my experience in the proper context, so the extreme effects that using shamanic technologies had on my life can be fully appreciated, please allow me to briefly describe my life prior to using DMT.

For most of my youth I grew up in a low-income housing project around a lot of negativity and low-vibrational culture that did not imbue respect for myself, women or other people into my consciousness. Then in the early 90's big money took over Hip-Hop music, influencing my culture with an abundance of degradation and negative values that affected me greatly since I began writing and performing Hip-Hop music at age 10, giving Hip-Hop much power over my own programming. I became a criminal, ran the streets with a negative crowd and began smoking tobacco, using marijuana and drinking alcohol by age 11.

I was taught many very bad habits that I brought into adulthood and that did not serve me well, even to the extent of being incarcerated more than once for living a crime-ridden lifestyle that involved drugs, guns, a (some might say) misogynistic view of women and zero respect for myself or anyone in my community. I was reckless, dishonest, lost and most people thought I was a lost cause doomed to a life of incarceration, pain and suffering.

Throughout my life, despite all the negativity and chaos, I was always a reader and always sought to innerstand the world better. I read books and tried my best to innerstand "God" and gain some sort of grip on spirituality.

I was raised into a religion that I didn't trust after being witness to abuses by some of the elders who should've been the ones who could be trusted the most. I didn't trust other religions that I read about being abused by the clergy and such, so I was pretty much lost with regard to spiritual education and had resigned to calling myself an atheist until God showed me who he or she was and what on Earth he or she might want for me or my life.

So that was the state of my life until at age 30 I was introduced to the term DMT and given some by a friend. I started to research it and immediately knew that I was on to something. It sat on my desk for 3 months while I spent 10 hours a day researching everything available online regarding this substance. I started with the documentary called "DMT: The Spirit Molecule" and just went into an approximately 90-day crash course on everything DMT-related. I didn't have a shaman at the time and knew no one who had any experience with DMT. Even the friend who gave it to me had only tried it once, and didn't have much more help for me other than a steady supply.

After about 3 months of research, I finally felt I had prepared myself enough to try it out and when I did, the very first thing that happened was I was "separated from my body." I watched the back of my head and torso as I "floated" backwards out of my body and the first thought that crossed my mind was, "I'M NOT MY BODY!".

I realized at that moment that if my thoughts are being created over "here" while my brain is in my body over "there", then my thoughts must in fact NOT be created in my brain. This meant to me that my consciousness must in fact exist in another dimension or on another plane separate from my brain and body which is where I was existing at that moment.

That realization changed everything for me. The most important thing it did was demonstrate to me that I'm much more than this body, much more than I've been led to believe and much more than I had access to in my normal cognitive state. I learned that day that I am a sacred and divine being, a spirit, a soul, a being with a body that can traverse the planes and unite with every atom in the universe at once. In effect, quite literally and figuratively, I am God.

I am God in every single sense of the word. It made 100%, complete and total sense to me at that point. I knew then that I would never doubt my divinity again, that I was worth more than I had been valuing myself at and that from that moment on I would be doing everything in my power to learn more about my divinity, move towards it and become the sacred God of a man I was born to be.

Yes, people CAN change. I did and you can, too.

Now I would like to state at this point, that extreme problems require extreme solutions. I was disconnected from my divinity and had some pretty extreme problems. I do innerstand that everyone isn't the negative person I had grown to become and might not require such extreme and radical solutions such as shamanic technologies to ascend to their higher selves and live a life with sacred and divine intention.

If you don't find that to be necessary then count yourself fortunate because many people do. If you feel you require such extreme measures to find yourself, in a world where it's so easy to become lost, then know that there is help and that help is becoming more and more accessible every day as shamanic technologies (or entheogens: chemical substances, typically of plant origin, that are ingested to produce a non-ordinary state of consciousness for religious or spiritual purposes) become legal and thus accessible in more and more places.

It must be stated that since DMT is a naturally occurring chemical in the human body, it only makes sense that there are natural ways to increase the level secreted into the bloodstream, thus allowing for access to higher states of awareness NATURALLY. Meditation, breath techniques and various rituals can allow for this and I advise reading up on ways to do this.

If you feel that you do require a shamanic technology to assist you in altering your programming then by all means seek out your local shaman. Do some research and ask for references. There are MANY scam artists, posers and users out there who would take a "sucker" for their money, but there are also many shamans and healers out there who are full of love and light to share with the world. Let your intuition be your guide in finding one. Then begin the journey of learning just how sacred you actually are.

If you don't know how sacred you are, how can you ever appreciate fully just how sacred your Goddess is?

CHAPTER 6: COMMUNICATE
HONESTLY AND FREQUENTLY

To love your Goddess more requires two seriously simple things, being honest with yourself and being honest with her. If you have trouble with either one of those then you won't be able to love her as completely as a Goddess should be loved. That means you're going to have to work on developing the ability to be honest with yourself, and then her as well.

No one likes to be lied to, not even unintentionally. In this society, we've been taught all too well how easy it is to put on a mask, become that mask and wear it all the time, sometimes for years.

The trouble with that lack of authenticity is that we forget who we are ourselves. Over time we begin to believe our own lies and the mask becomes our identity. That, my friend, is becoming lost. That is becoming someone else who you are not, and in all honesty that requires a great deal more of your time and energy to maintain than it would to simply be authentic.

The main benefit to being authentic, though, is that your anxiety level drops dramatically since you're never worried about "being found out". If your word is unimpeachable then you can't be impeached. No one can say and be able to prove that you are being dishonest. No one can call you out for being a fraud. No one can catch you in a lie. No one can blackmail you and hold you hostage with your fraud.

Simply and plainly, the truth is that honesty is in fact always the best policy. It always has been and always will be. There is no way around this one. You simply MUST learn to be 100% authentic if you would learn to love her more. You simply MUST learn to be 100% authentic if you would desire to attract the same in a lifelong companion.

The thing about truth that has proved constant since time began is that it has a way of always coming to light. The old axiom holds true because it just does. You don't have to search very far into your own memory to find examples of this yourself. So for your own sake and to save yourself and your woman a lot of heartache, stress and argument, do all that you can from this moment on to correct any lies told, remove any masks and begin to live a life that is completely and utterly 100% authentic. She will love you more for it and you will be showing her that you love her by the very act of being authentic.

Once you have the authentic part down, learn to communicate truth to your Goddess in ways that demonstrate your desire to be forthcoming about things, but with regard for her emotions, ego and self-esteem. We all want to be told the truth, but we also don't want people to be brutal and disregard our feelings. So talk to your Goddess about what's on your mind, especially if there are any issues in the relationship that need to be addressed. Be open, honest and intelligent in your presentation of the truth. By all means, though, tell her the truth.

Set aside time from the daily grind to actually communicate with your Goddess. Schedule some quiet time where responsibility, kids, food, phones, friends, electronics and such are not in the way of uninterrupted communication time with you and your Goddess. Chances are there are things on her mind and yours that could come out, be discussed and make the relationship run more smoothly.

CHAPTER 7: LISTEN-HEAR-CONSIDER

How many times have you heard a woman say, "He never LISTENS to me!"? Well, chances are if she said it to you, then you might be a victim of a quite frequently diagnosed psychological condition called ioeaotoitis (pronounced "YOU ARE MESSING UP BADLY") known more commonly as in-one-ear-and-out-the-other-itis. Sad to say that when this diagnosis is valid, it can lead to serious relationship problems including but not limited to unnecessary arguments, verbal abuse, fights, distrust, neglect, loneliness, diminishing intimacy, snuggleless nights and worst of all (for everyone involved) no sex.

Here's the good news: IT CAN BE TREATED! Phew, right? I mean, it would be a shame if there was no way to remedy that one, huh? Well, for those of you suffering from ioeaotoitis, it's fortunate for you that you are able to treat this condition yourself without a medical doctor or Goddess-forbid, a shrink. It does require some time and effort and the only pill you'll have to swallow is your pride, but I'm sure you can fix this and be back to optimal relationship health a lot sooner than you might think.

The first step in being rid of ioeaotoitis is to check your ears for waxy buildup and be sure that your hearing is at an optimal level. If the instrument used to receive sound has an issue then you might simply be deaf and at that point you and your Goddess would need to learn sign language. If, however, you ears are wax-free and work great then you will need to proceed with the following procedures in this order:

1. Give your Goddess a big hug.
2. Humbly apologize to her for your self-inflicted illness and encourage her with your desire to heal the condition.

3. Ask her for her assistance and patience as you work through the reprogramming process.
4. Give her another big hug.
5. Grab a notebook and pen or pencil.
6. Give her another big hug.
7. Ask her what's on her mind then shut up and listen, writing down anything important you want to rebut, rebuke, remark on, question, fact check or debate.
8. Let her finish.
9. Give her another big hug.
10. Kiss her on the forehead where the third eye (or pineal gland) is located.
11. Thank her for taking the time out of her day to keep you abreast of her latest thought processes.
12. Inform her that you would like to schedule another meeting soon where you might discuss some of the things she mentioned, but only after you've had some time to let things marinate and seriously consider what she said, how you feel about any of it, and what your proper response should be after that contemplation period is complete.
13. Give her another big hug then walk away.
14. As soon as you get the chance, read over the list you made and give some serious thought to what she said, making notes where you feel her statements were in error, unjustified, incorrect, unreasonable, emotionally-charged, ignorant, unfair, etc.
15. Write down an outline of the things you'd like to discuss in your next meeting and then prepare yourself to dialogue about those points.

Now you may be thinking, "I don't need paper for that, I can remember it all in my head and win any argument with her hands down.", but if that's your first thought, your condition may be worse than ioeaotoitis. That mode of thinking usually indicates that a man has a completely different, but also quite common, diagnosis known as inmeditis (pronounced "NOBODY WINS ARGUMENTS, YOU BOTH LOSE") but more commonly referred to as I-need-my-ego-downsized-itis.

Inmeditis-sufferers exhibit symptoms such as erroneously believing a relationship is a struggle between two people rather than a partnership between two people who, as a team, are supposed to be working TOGETHER towards a common goal. Inmeditis-sufferers are known to sabotage their relationships with spiteful behavior, distancing behavior and the breeding of distrust. If you suffer from inmeditis, a shamanic intervention may be necessary. Find one immediately.

Now, if ioeaotoitis is your only issue, you have completed the 15 steps above, you've determined you don't have inmeditis and you want to love your Goddess more, then go over the list you made one last time before your meeting and approach the meeting as if you're meeting with yourself and you have to discuss these things with your EQUAL.

Every relationship is different, every couple thinks differently and there are many variables that make a complete manual to deal with ioeaotoitis literally impossible. However, I can guarantee that if you approach this meeting humbly, respectfully, lovingly, considerately, calmly, intelligently and in the spirit of teamwork, without the need to WIN (against your teammate) then the likelihood that you have cured (or are on the way to curing) your ioeaotoitis and the very act of approaching this meeting in such a way will unequivocally demonstrate to your Goddess that you are taking charge of ridding yourself of ioeaotoitis. That fact alone, being shown to her without ulterior motive, will usually be enough to inject a huge dose of cohesion back into your bond. Repeat this procedure for every episode of ioeaotoitis in the future.

It is wise to note that whoever walks away from the meeting having "won over" the other with the points they made is immaterial to the object of this procedure. The object of this procedure is to work TOGETHER on something, not argue about who's right. Team work makes the dream work. If it doesn't then you're on the wrong team and need to read Chapter 1 of this book.

Anyone seeking to enhance their listening skills more might want to explore 40 year counseling veteran James C. Petersen's "Why Don't We Listen Better? Communicating & Connecting in Relationships". The title says it all. You'll be better for reading this book. Just do it.

CHAPTER 8: TRUST HER

This should go without saying, but in the world we live in, nothing can be left to assumption. Many tend to assume that when two people are in a relationship they automatically trust one another. However, this is far from the common experience. Too many people do not completely trust their significant others.

If you do not trust yours then I suggest you go back to Chapter 1 and read it again, because If you haven't chosen THE ONE, then your problems are bigger than trust. Yes, it's really that simple, that short and that sweet. Trust her. Just do it.

CHAPTER 9: DO THE WORK

They say relationships require a lot of hard work. I contend that this is false. Now before you go calling me names and assassinating my character, hear me out and think about what I'm going to say, because I'm sure that by the end of this book you'll agree with my contention that relationships do not "have" to require hard work.

Now, notice I didn't say that there is no work to be done. There is definitely always work to do. The difference is that the work required is usually personal self work that the individuals involved need to perform on themselves, rather than anything in particular about the actual relationship that requires moving a mountain.

Oftentimes people come to us broken, bruised, traumatized, neglected, unloved, vengeful, vindictive, etc. Many of these issues are hidden behind a mask of ego, pride and/or shame. Masks are what allows for relationship mismatches to occur since two masks meeting and forcing a connection have nothing to do with the two people behind the masks having the slightest thing in common. Even one person wearing a mask will lead to a similar mismatch with a partner who is being authentic.

In light of the information presented in this chapter so far, doing the work is something that each individual needs to take upon oneself to explore, executing any necessary functions, until one is on stable ground, standing in one's own authenticity and able to truly offer oneself to another as a whole being, complete on one's own and ready to enter a transparent bond of friendship, trust, love and partnership.

This is where you must analyze yourself and ask honest and hard questions:

Am I an honest person? With others? With myself? Do I truly love myself? Do I love others? Do I give as much as I take? Am I considerate of others? Am I selfish? Is my ego/pride a barrier for authentic connection with others? Does anyone "really" know me? Do I "really" know myself? Am I wearing a mask? Who am I? What am I? What makes me "me"? What could I do to be a better person? How could I be more honest with myself? With others? How can I remove this mask and be more authentic? Would I want to be in a relationship with me if all truth was exposed? Why or why not? What changes would I need to make to become someone I can love? Others can love?

Answering all of those questions "honestly" is the first step in "doing the work". The next step in doing the work is tweaking (or overhauling if necessary, as will be in some cases) yourself, then asking all the questions again. Then tweaking yourself, then asking all the questions again. Then tweaking yourself, then asking all the questions again. Rinse, repeat, rinse, repeat, until you know that the work is being done, realize that the work will never be complete, and have successfully made doing the work a permanent part of your personal programming.

Doing the work is a personal journey that each individual must take responsibility for. A wise couple innerstands this and will hold space for each other to do the work on self while simultaneously doing the work on self. You can't fix people, but you can give guidance, instruction, wisdom and patience to someone who is becoming more responsible, accountable and who is doing the work. If your Goddess is holding space for you to do the work then do the work. Do the work. Do the work! Then, do some more work.

Don't you ever think there is no work to be done. The one fact that will remain constant as long as you inhabit a human body is that you will never be "perfect". There will always be upward movement to conquer, enlightenment to be had, growth to move through, shadows to shed light on, mountains to move and new ways of loving to learn.

Pushing down the road towards perfection might never make you a perfect being, but might make you the perfect match for your Goddess who may only need the encouragement that you are actually doing the work. A little encouragement can go a long way in a relationship. Do the work, until you leave this place. That's the best advice you will ever hear in your life. You would be wise to take heed.

One other thing, don't expect doing the work to be easy. If it was easy this chapter would be called "Doing The Play". Just do it.

CHAPTER 10: COOK HER DELICIOUS, NUTRITIOUS MEALS

[DISCLAIMER: This chapter may contrast with many people's views on food, so please bear with me, take what you will and leave what you don't want. Remember these are simply ideas from my own experience, meant to inspire and are by no means absolute.]

They say that the way to a man's heart is through his stomach. While that may hold true for many men, the same could be said for many women as well. I would go so far as to say that the way to a woman's heart is through her waistline. I say this for two reasons. The first is that her stomach is somewhere beneath her waistline, and the second reason is that most women would prefer to maintain or lessen their waistline.

The industry selling healthy food is growing exponentially and, with it, the amount of delicious recipes for preparing healthy food. I've personally had some wholly plant-based meals with no processed food involved that tasted just as good, if not better, than any not-so-healthy meals I've consumed. Vegetarian and vegan fare is getting more and more delicious as more chefs, consumers and industries focus on healthy food.

In this day and age, the age of drone pizza delivery, it's easy to order a meal via a smartphone app and have just about anything you can imagine being consumed by humans delivered to your front door in a matter of minutes. I mean anything. The problem with this level of technology and convenience is that it opens the door for all kinds of abuse, one being abuse by way of neglecting "proper" nutrition in lieu of convenience and taste bud gratification.

It's not difficult to innerstand why Americanized culture has a serious problem with obesity. For one, Americanized culture has a serious problem with convenience and gratification. These two things combined have contributed to a gross overindulgence of fast food and nationwide malnutrition of epidemic proportions..

Most people think of malnutrition as something that only occurs in places where there is lack of food in general, however study after study has shown that a staggering number of people, in what we call industrialized societies, are being malnourished while eating costly meals that the FDA has approved could be sold as "food".

Well, it turns out that the FDA, as well as other similar government agencies involved with the food and drug industries, seem to be unable to avoid approving many foods/drugs/chemicals (these three are one and the same, there really is no difference) that harm the human body and may lack, or even prevent the body from being able to absorb (i.e.; gluten), the proper vital nutrients that *are* actually being consumed.

There are many examples of faulty substance approvals that can be easily reviewed by using a search engine to find lawsuits aimed at the FDA and food and drug companies for punitive damages, specifically cases related to harm done to consumers, plants and livestock by products which our government watchdogs approved as safe for use and/or consumption, in many cases without adhering to proper protocol. Proper protocol would include peer-reviewed INDEPENDENT safety studies rather than merely "studies" paid for by elements of the industries involved who would benefit from the product's approval, and may have lobbied for the approval via legal or back door bribery means.

I'll leave it up to you and your own research to decide how much conspiracy within the food and drug industries is going on behind your back, but I can promise you one thing: no matter how much you think you know, you have a lot to learn.

After 15 years of personal research (that started when my

daughter got 4 vaccines at once when she was one year old and "became autistic" within 24 hours) and many days of spending 10-16 hours of food and drug research time in front of a computer screen, it has become irrevocably clear to me that we are being attacked. We are being covertly attacked by unscrupulous, greedy corporations that conspire among themselves to make money harming us, then make even more money by offering solutions to the very health problems their products cause. These are referred to as silent weapons for quiet wars.

RNA interference technology is one excellent example of a quiet weapon since most of you reading this have never heard of it, innerstand it, or would ever question how it might be (if not already) used against us to cause harm to our bodies. I would suggest to those desiring to love themselves and their loved ones more to put some serious time into educating themselves about diet, nutrition and how to source and prepare healthy food that will bring life, rather than harm, to the human body.

Putting poison in your body is not loving yourself. Putting poison into the body of your Goddess or any one else you love is not loving them. There aren't many adults in the modern world who can honestly say that they have "no idea" how harmful fast foods and junk foods are. Not many can say they aren't aware that it's exponentially healthier for you to eat produce rather than anything else. So buying or preparing unhealthy substances for consumption is knowingly harming and not loving someone. Period.

If you "allow" your Goddess to consume, or worse yet prepare for her with your own hands, harmful food without lovingly educating her on the harm being done, you are not loving her. You are not loving yourself by eating it either. Educating yourself about the current state of diet and nutrition knowledge should be enough incentive to cause you to want to take it upon yourself to prepare, or orchestrate the preparation of, healthy, life-giving food to your Goddess and yourself. It is up to you to take the initiative for yourself and for your Goddess if she isn't already well-educated on nutrition. Always be the instigator of healthy conversations regarding the latest scientific research on nutrition and diet.

Chances are that your Goddess will receive your enthusiasm for proper diet as loving her more. This will make your connection stronger, her trust for you grow and your relationship healthier overall since you'll likely spend more time in the kitchen together learning about and preparing new dishes together. A healthy diet will make your sex life better by giving you both more energy and vitality. It will boost your general health and more than likely add longevity to both of your lives and the life of the relationship. She can view this in no other way than you loving her (and yourself) more, which is sure to come with some perks.

CHAPTER 11: READ A BOOK ABOUT LOVE WITH HER

There are lots of ways to learn wisdom with regard to relationships. This book is written in hopes that most will learn what not to do before they make all the mistakes I made and witnessed being made in my two failed marriages and other failed relationships. It's always best to learn from the wisdom of others if possible, but if you must make mistakes on your own then so be it. However, you may want a gauge to measure your behavior by, simply so you can know how far off track you are, and one of the best ways to do that is to read what some of the foremost experts on love and relationships have to say on the matter.

So here I've compiled a list of some of my favorites which also happen to be some of the most revered, most reviewed, most loved and best-selling books on the market about love relationships and how to maintain them for maximum satisfaction by all parties involved. There is more than one book here that can help make your relationship better in more ways than one, but feel free to read them all:

- "The 5 Love Languages: The Secret to Love That Lasts" by Gary Chapman
- "Emotionally Focused Couple Therapy for Dummies" by Brent Bradley and James Furrow
- "Men Are From Mars, Women Are From Venus: Practical Guide for Improving Communication" by John Gray
- "The New Rules of Marriage" by Terrence Real
- "I Love You But I Don't Trust You: The Complete Guide to Restoring Trust in Your Relationship" by Mira Kirshenbaum
- "The ADHD Effect on Marriage" by Melissa Orlov
- "Deal Breakers: When to Work On a Relationship and When to Walk Away" by Dr. Bethany Marshall

- "Love and Respect: The Love She Most Desires; The Respect He Desperately Needs" by Emerson Eggerichs
- "Getting the Love You Want" by Harville Hendrix and Helen LaKelly
- "Mindful Relationship Habits: 25 Practices for Couples to Enhance Intimacy, Nurture Closeness, and Grow a Deeper Connection" by SJ Scott and Barrie Davenport
- "The Seven Principles for Making Marriage Work: A Practical Guide From the Country's Foremost Relationship Expert" by John Gottman, PhD
- "Crucial Conversations: Tools for Talking When the Stakes Are High" by Kerry Patterson, Joseph Grenny, Ron McMillan, Al Switzler
- "Couple Skills: Making Your Relationship Work" by Matthew McKay PhD and Patrick Fanning
- "The Art of Loving" by Erich Fromm
- "47 Little Love Boosters For a Happy Marriage: Connect and Instantly Deepen Your Bond No Matter How Busy You Are" by Marko Petkovic
- "The Relationship Cure: A 5-Step Guide to Strengthening Your Marriage, Family, and Friendships" by John Gottman
- "Hold Me Tight: Seven Conversations for a Lifetime of Love" by Sue Johnson
- "Conscious Loving: The Journey to Co-Commitment" by Gay Hendricks and Kathlyn Hendricks
- "Love Is Never Enough: How Couples Can Overcome Misunderstanding" by Aaron T. Beck M.D.
- "The Science of Happily Ever After: What Really Matters in the Quest for Enduring Love" by Ty Tashiro
- "Make Love Last A Lifetime" by Barbara De Angelis
- "Attached: The New Science of Adult Attachment and How It Can Help You Find -- And Keep -- Love" by Amir Levine and Rachel S.F. Heller
- "Mating in Captivity: Unlocking Erotic Intelligence" by Esther Perel
- "Conflict-Free Living: How to Build Healthy

Relationships for Life" by Joyce Meyer

Read these books on your own or preferably with your partner. One thing is for sure, any God that reads these books with his Goddess will definitely be doing the work, loving her more and letting her know that she is being loved more. Your Goddess deserves no less, so pick a title that resonates and dive in.

CHAPTER 12: HELP HER TO DOMESTICATE YOU

One of the worst things that parents can do is raise children that are completely unfamiliar with work traditionally delegated to the opposite sex. It's amazing how many people grow up with both parents, but don't learn basic domestic and survival skills from both parents.

I'm sure there will be some who disagree, but I contend that, in addition to what is traditionally taught to children, males should learn how to cook, do laundry and care for infants, and females should learn how to change tires and oil, mow grass and put together furniture. My reasoning isn't that you might spend all your days indulging in tasks usually delegated to the opposite sex, but you might have to spend "some" time doing so. Wouldn't it be nice to have the skills already if you found yourself living alone one day and were forced by necessity to perform all these functions on your own?

In four decades I've seen some things. I've seen men almost starve or eat some of the most ludicrous, half-cooked concoctions because they didn't know their way around a kitchen. I've seen men bleach dark clothes doing laundry wrong and burn clothes they attempted to iron. I've seen babies in diapers that were so sagging with crap that I wanted to literally slap the supervising male that should have changed the diaper hours ago but "didn't know how".

On the other hand, I've seen a woman wait in a car for three or for hours on a male to arrive and change her tire when she could've done it in 15 minutes and been on her way had she only been instructed on how easy it actually is to accomplish. I've seen a woman look at a screwdriver like an alien ray gun that might disintegrate her body if she touched it, as if possessing mechanical inclination might be a mortal sin.

Don't get me wrong, I innerstand that men are, by nature, on average physically stronger than women, however, there are plenty of women who change tires and plenty of men who change diapers and no one has ever died from either of those revolutionary acts.

Get over the stereotypes. Get over the programming. Get over the silliness. We all need help and more than likely the person closest to us and most capable of assisting us is our significant other.

One of the sexiest things about a man, polled women have consistently revealed, is domestic capability. There seems to be something about a man who knows his way around the kitchen and/or broom closet that does it for women in a way that sweaty, mechanic-oiled hands just can't do. There's something about a man who knows how to burp a baby that usually leads to more babies. I'm sure you get the picture.

This goes for women, too, since you haven't met a woman you found attractive who didn't turn you on even more by demonstrating that she could put a new alternator belt on her car or light the pilot on the oven. But I digress. This chapter is about domesticating men so let's focus on men.

If you are unaware of the intricacies of the domestic workings of a household, you would go far in loving your Goddess more by educating yourself more in this area. You can do this on your own, but might find it easier to learn from your Goddess, if she's capable herself and so inclined to instruct you.

Receiving instruction from your Goddess on housework or domestic affairs traditionally "relegated" to women will do wonders for your love life, will show your Goddess that you see her as an equal and will scream to her in a very loud way that you desire to love her more. Trust me, just do it.

CHAPTER 13: CALL HER JUST TO SAY "I LOVE YOU"

As of the writing of this book world famous R&B singer Stevie Wonder's most popular song "I Just Called To Say I Love You" (1984 UMG/ASCAP) has 104,695,877 views on YouTube. That's 1/10 of a BILLION views for a song in English.

According to a Babbel Magazine article found at www.babbel.com/en/magazine/how-many-people-speak-english-and-where-is-it-spoken:

*"Out of the world's approximately 7.5 billion inhabitants, **1.5 billion** speak English — that's 20% of the Earth's population. However, most of those people aren't native English speakers. About 360 million people speak English as their first language."*

Now if I'm doing the math correctly, this means that there's been a Youtube download of this song at least once for roughly 7% of the total English speaking population around the world! SEVEN PERCENT of people who can innerstand its words have heard this song. It might not sound like a lot, but as a recording artist who's released music for years, I know the industry and let me assure you that 7% of the English speakers in the world hearing a song means it's POP-U-LAR!

That percentage didn't even include the countless audio and video streaming platforms online. Only Youtube. It's difficult to estimate the total audio and video downloads and streams of this song, but any expert guesstimator would put it in the billions without a doubt.

That, my friends, is one powerful song. A powerful notion. It must be a powerful thing to do. To call someone just to say

"I love you".

When is the last time you called your Goddess just to say "I love you"? How do you think that would make her feel? Do you think it might make her feel like you are loving her more? Then what are you waiting for? Mark your page in this book, put it somewhere safe from fire, water and pets, then call her. Right now.

Just do it.

CHAPTER 14: KISSES AND HUGS

It goes without saying that as social creatures all humans need intimacy on some level and your Goddess is no exception. Chances are that the Goddess in a relationship with you desires as much intimacy as possible to reinforce the safety she feels by simply being called your Goddess. She desires affection to reinforce the bond of sensual love and sacred romance between you two that can grow stale and disconnected if only watered fleetingly and when it's convenient or when there's nothing else to do at a given time.

Don't let the romance grow stale. That's what this book is about. Keeping the love rich, nourishing and full of power and energy that you both can feed off in your daily lives while away from each other at work, school, etc.

Romance has to be watered and fed with life and love. With careful attention, planning and following through, smart couples make time for intimacy. Smarter couples make time for intimacy AND also steal as much EXTRA time for intimacy as they possibly can because they see it as one of the driving forces of their relationship.

Kissing is what sparked the fire in the first place, so when the fire burns down to coals, kissing might just be the thing you need to get the fire blazing again. Your Goddess wants you to kiss her like there's no tomorrow, then kiss her the same way when tomorrow comes. When you stop kissing her like you mean it, then she thinks you don't mean it. She needs to know you mean it. It would show her that you want to love her more. So kiss her. Kiss her hard. Kiss her fiercely. Kiss her like an animal if that's what she likes, but by all means, my brother, use your mouth to make love to your Goddess's mouth once in a while and I assure you, she will feel a lot more loved.

And don't let me get started on HUGS!

Virginia Satir, a notable family therapist once stated, "We need four hugs a day for survival. We need 8 hugs a day for maintenance. We need 12 hugs a day for growth." How many hugs per day does your Goddess need to feel more loved? Start today and give her LOTS of hugs!

An article at http://www.healthline.com/health/hugging-benefits/ claims that hugs are responsible for the following:
- reducing stress by showing support
- possibly helping protect against illness
- possibly helping boost heart health
- possibly helping induce happiness
- possibly helping reduce fears
- possibly helping reduce pain
- helping communicate with others
- certainly strengthening the bond of any relationship
- certainly bringing more intimacy to any situation
- certainly making a Goddess feel more loved

Okay, I admit that I added the last three, but that doesn't mean they aren't actual, factual truths. What does Health Line have that I don't? Look, the bottom line here, fellas, is that kisses and hugs are a necessary, mandatory, paramount, un-do-without-able part of a romantic relationship that has any chance of surviving over the long haul. So if you value your relationship with your Goddess then you might want to check your kissandhugometer to make sure you're meeting your quota. If you're not, then get on it asap! Just do it.

CHAPTER 15: WRITE HER POETRY

Hey there! Yeah you! Edgar Allan Slow...lol. Just kidding, I know you're not slow or you wouldn't be reading this encyclopedia of Goddess-retention information, now would you? Well, now that we've established how awesome you are, let's get to the point of this chapter.

Every man isn't Edgar Allan Poe or Robert Frost. Hell, some men really suck at roses are red, violets are blues. The fact remains, however, that no matter what your level of poetry writing ability, the very act of using your own creativity, time and energy to manifest something unique for your Goddess is a powerful act of showing her your desire to love her more.

The biggest fear I think people have with poetry and attempting to write it, is the belief that it has to rhyme and they may not be good at rhyming. Here's the thing, though. Poetry doesn't have to rhyme. EVER. There are poets who never rhyme.

There are poets who write two-line poems and there are poets who write 200 line poems. There are poets who write poems in the shape of an apple or a bird or some other simple shape just to be cute and graphically artistic.

The biggest ingredient in what makes a poem likable, at least from my personal perspective as a poet, is how unique it is. If you tell your truth in a unique way that I haven't seen before, there's a much higher chance that I'll find it interesting, like it and remember it. Use that as a rule when writing your truth on paper in poetry form for your Goddess and I'm sure she'll be impressed with your effort.

Ask yourself "How can I use poetry to tell my truth of desiring to love my Goddess more?" Start writing whatever comes to mind and simply let your pen flow until ideas start to crystallize. The more you practice this sort of thing, the better you get. It's really not difficult at all to write poetry, so I bet that the more you practice writing it the better you get at it, and probably a lot quicker than you might have as a child since you're much smarter and more educated than you were back in elementary school when your third grade teacher tried to get you to do it.

If you try and you're having trouble coming up with ideas, there's nothing at all wrong with reading other poets' work online to find ideas and inspiration for your next poem. The bottom line here is that EVERY Goddess is simply in love with the idea of a God writing poetry about her. That is a fact of life in every culture, every language, every creed. Trust me. Just try it. At the very least you'll write a silly poem that will make her laugh. Every Goddess likes to laugh, and you know what they say, "if you can make her laugh…".

Just do it.

CHAPTER 16: PICK OUT AN OUTFIT THAT YOU WOULD LOVE TO SEE HER IN

One thing you can be sure of in life is that women are like peacocks. No I don't mean they have beaks and eat insects, but rather that they are fond of being seen as beautiful and being told or shown that others think that their "feathers" are beautiful. That's why the fashion industry is so dynamic and enormous.

This doesn't mean that every woman wants to flaunt her stuff to everyone. Many women only want to show their figure or beauty to their God. However, out in public, there is great demand to be the trophy on your arm, especially to other women, and if your Goddess isn't an exception to this rule, then you could love her more by being sensitive to her needs regarding her self-image and self-esteem.

She needs to know that she is pleasing to your eyes, and no matter what her physical disposition, if you truly love her inside and out then you will see every part of her as beautiful, no matter what anyone else, including the fashion industry, says or thinks.

You are your Goddess's first line of defense against the media and all it's consumerist magic attempting to make your Goddess and every other Goddess feel less than perfect, less than beautiful and less than enough. You are the most powerful weapon she has against those attacks. If she doesn't feel beautiful, it's very likely that she wasn't defended properly by a man she put her trust in to do so.

An act as simple as picking out an outfit for your Goddess to wear and having it laid out for her when she walks in, maybe with a little note on it that says, "I'd love to see you in this tonight! xoxo", might go a long way in boosting your Goddess's self image, especially after being exposed to a society and social media that bombards her with negative self-imagery all day every day, attacking her psyche with attempts to make her feel like she needs to buy this or that to be as beautiful as the celebrity women "all men want", maybe even her God.

When she walks into her home and, instead of finding you watching some sexy celebrity female on TV or social media, her God was rather home fantasizing about what she will look like in a certain outfit, so much that he had to lay it out for her to make sure she wears it, she will be sure to feel loved more by her God. She will not only feel loved more, but will love you even more for it. Don't ever stop picking out a sexy outfit that you'd like to see her in.

Nothing makes a woman feel as sexy as giving a fashion show to her man and seeing desire in his eyes. When your Goddess steps in from her closet holding a dress up in front of her and asks for your opinion, give it to her and be honest. But go a step further and offer to step into the closet with her and help her decide. "Hey baby, what happened to that one outfit you wore that night we got crazy? You know the one we had to send to the cleaners?", is always a good way to start a great night. Closets can be FUN! But don't take my word for it. Just do it.

CHAPTER 17: NEVER STOP DATING HER

Once you've helped her pick out the outfit she will look the most stunning in, it's time to take your Goddess out on a date. An actual DATE date. Open every door, hold her hand, tell her how gorgeous she looks, introduce her to people as "my Goddess", pay for everything and smile when you do so (even if it hurts your pockets a little bit) because her pedestal is worth it. Men will take a new female on a date and spend absurd amounts of money trying to impress her when they don't even really know her, or if she might be the right fit. How much more would you spend on the woman you have chosen to be your Goddess and put up on a sacred pedestal for the rest of your lives?

Women are very intelligent, much more so than many will allow men to see, since that can work as a protection of sorts in this patriarchal society where many men still in this day and age believe women are inferior to men. (Absurd I know, but sad and true.) If you think that your intelligent Goddess can't recall the exact amounts you spent on things in the past that should be a lot less important than her, then you have no idea what game you're playing and what the rules are, my friend.

When you go and spend $500 on a video game console and $50-$70 for "another" video game, but complain about spending $100 to take her to a nice restaurant for a healthy meal, it doesn't say to her that you desire to love her more. When you pay $200 for "another" pair of shoes, but complain about paying $20 to valet the car so she doesn't have to walk 3-4 blocks in heels that she wore to look sexy for you, it doesn't demonstrate that you desire to love her more.

The problem with some people is that they get comfortable in relationships and forget that every single day you have to make a choice to choose your Goddess again and again. That's what keeps the love alive, choosing her. When you first chose her, you took her out on a date, and you probably spent more than you do when you've taken her out lately. Why do you think she would want to feel less special now? Think about that then buy her a dozen roses for your next date, just because. She will more than likely see that as your desire to love her more.

In other words, don't expect a wife experience at a girlfriend price. Just do it.

CHAPTER 18: HOLD HER HAND IN PUBLIC

Holding your Goddess's hand is not something you want to reserve only for dates or special occasions. Hand-holding is not only for show. Holding her hand should be something you enjoy and see as a privilege that you wear proudly like a badge of honor. Holding her hand should never feel like a chore. If it does then you're doing something wrong. And it's more than likely a wrong way of perceiving things.

When your Goddess reaches for your hand in public, it may not be because she's insecure. It might just be that she wants the world to know who has claimed her and who she has surrendered to. That is a gift to you, and you would be wise to treat it as such.

If you are having internal thoughts about not wanting to hold her hand, think of hand-holding as you would think of wearing wedding rings. It's a signal to the world that this sacred bond is protected, that you have conquered each other's defense mechanisms, met all standards that needed to be met, chose each other and are protecting the divine union between a God and Goddess with a public display of affection that is a universal sign to all, saying, "we are both spoken for".

If you are truly in love with, devoted to and desiring to give more love to your Goddess, then hold her hand. Hold it firmly, but gently and caress it. Always let her know that having her hand in yours is a pleasure that you wouldn't like to do without. She will no doubt correctly view that as your desire to love her more.

CHAPTER 19: BREAK DOWN YOUR WALLS (AND HERS)

A woman will only show you her bad girl when she believes in your good man.

Too many men have been programmed by Hollywood, religion, pop culture and patriarchal culture in general to believe that men who show vulnerability, especially to a woman are weak and/ or feminine, thus less desirable. In all actuality, the complete opposite is true.

A Goddess appreciates the trust inherent in the act of her God confiding his pain, hurt, traumas, wounds, worries or concerns to her. For one, it builds the bond of trust and cohesion between them and it also offers the Goddess a chance to be the strong one and hold space for her God to heal and be protected. This exchange is an essential element to a complete relationship between two human beings who allow each other to be their true authentic selves in every way.

There is nothing feminine about crying and there isn't one person reading this book who hasn't cried multiple times in their life. It's really silly to even suggest that you would never cry. If, Heaven forbid, your mother or father died in front of you right now, are you "man enough" to not cry? Let's be real, most of us would be sobbing, not because we're soft, but because we're humans with emotions just like everyone else.

If a man is afraid to cry, it's usually an indication that he is concealing pain deep down somewhere that if disturbed might come gushing out with unstoppable force. I invite men to explore those old wounds, some from early childhood, some from bloodlines past, all needing to eventually be faced head on and dealt with.

There is an old saying, "The bill must come due." Wise men choose to face the shadows with light and move through the difficult work that must be done to elevate to higher states of consciousness and higher bonds in our relationships. Many Goddesses are able to assist their Gods in moving through and healing pain. I've personally had more than one woman from my past and even present assist me with healing trauma from my past and I'm a better man for allowing them to see me cry and for allowing them to hold space for me to be human.

They trusted me more and opened up to me even more after that, so don't be afraid to break down your walls of defense and allow the person closest to you, your main teammate, to kiss your wounds and help you heal. Becoming vulnerable to your Goddess is one of the most intimate things you can do and one of the most powerful ways to demonstrate your trust in her. That act in itself can only show her that you desire to love her more. Just do it.

CHAPTER 20: PROTECT HER

Your Goddess is putting much, if not all of her heart, mind and body in your care with the expectation that you love her enough to offer her protection, safety, loyalty, fidelity, trust and emotional nourishment among other things. Too many men have allowed Hollywood and other forms of low-vibrational entertainment (programming) to erode the fabric of true love's tapestry and undermine what it means to offer real protection to a Goddess.

This chapter is to be referred to from time to time, as a checklist to compare your current situation and mindset to, in order to be clear and sure that you are not neglecting to protect your Goddess in ways that might not be so clear to every male. Too many men forget that as males in a patriarchal society, we must be the defenders not only of our Goddess's heart, but also of her rights, privileges, honor, wants and needs. This is in addition to the defense of our own.

She trusts you to protect her, so don't let her down. If you are contributing in any way (even in the slightest) to any of the following listed behaviors, you are not protecting your Goddess:

- harming or disrespecting your Goddess in any way is not protecting her
- manipulating your Goddess in any way is not protecting her
- berating (especially bullying) your Goddess, especially in front of other people is not protecting her
- making decisions that affect you both without consulting her is not protecting her
- having sexual contact with anyone other than your Goddess is not protecting her
- having a non-sexual but "emotional" private relationship with someone you find attractive (especially without her knowledge and/or consent) is not protecting

her

- ❏ flirting with or seeking attention from other women on social media is not protecting her
- ❏ indulging in porn without her knowledge or consent is not protecting her
- ❏ letting anyone or anything shake the pedestal you hold her up on is not protecting her
- ❏ Complaining, especially to someone you find attractive, about your Goddess is not protecting her
- ❏ telling anyone your Goddess's secrets is not protecting her
- ❏ emotionally abusing your Goddess in any way is not protecting her
- ❏ putting any passion, work, hobby, game, person, etc., above the relationship with your Goddess is not protecting her
- ❏ being dishonest or keeping secrets about pretty much anything other than a surprise gift or event is not protecting her
- ❏ withholding finances or financial information while expecting your Goddess to divulge hers is not protecting her
- ❏ refusing to seek help when things are a hopeless mess is not protecting her
- ❏ not doing the work is not protecting her

If you feel guilty about any of the above actions, you have an area that needs attention and you should refer to one of the books in chapter 11 for further guidance. Your Goddess deserves your protection, not only from others, but also from you and the male ego. If you're not going to protect her, then someone else will. Never forget that.

CHAPTER 21: STARE AT CLOUDS AND STARS WITH HER

It is vital to a healthy relationship that you and your Goddess are comfortable and find enjoyment in spending time together when there is absolutely no agenda but being together and passing time in each other's company. This should flow easily and should be something you both desire.

Lying on your backs and staring up at clouds or stars are excellent circumstances for this type of thing, but let your creativity go berserk on this one. This is a huge world with a fafillion ways to pass time with your beloved Goddess in enjoyable ways. The purpose of this concept is to not be bored, but to be inspired by beautiful things that will spark new conversations that allow you both to explore your highest versions of yourselves and the highest version of your relationship.

Many couples attempt to do this via television or other forms of electronic stimulation that implement Hollywoodish forms of media. I HIGHLY advise against this, since the vibration of much of that type of entertainment is not about entertainment, but rather to make you feel unhappy about your current state of existence so that you are compelled to spend hard-earned money on something you absolutely do not need to be happy.

My recommendation for spending this kind of time together is to go somewhere relating to nature and it's magic and beauty, somewhere that your lives, minds and your relationship will have more opportunity to be infused with this magic and beauty. Infusing your relationship with magic and beauty is the only way to have a magical, beautiful relationship that you both will wake up to every single day wondering how you ever even lived before having each other.

Those are the relationships that last 50-60 even 80 years, all the while maintaining a level of magic that misaligned couples can only dream of. You can be that couple. You can have that magic and beauty in your relationship. You won't find it on television or online. You will most likely find the best inspiration for that somewhere with a huge body of water and not many people or somewhere with a lot of trees and plenty of wild animals. Somewhere that your magic, and your Goddess's magic can shine through to each other and you can both be yourselves and be inspired by nature to remember that you are both divine, you are both sacred and that you both honor that with your full focus and attention. That is love. Just do it.

CHAPTER 22: LEAVE HER LOVE NOTES EVERYWHERE

One thing that has been a constant in human society as far back as the record shows is that people have written poetry for their objects of affection. This photo is on record as the oldest love note (a love poem actually) in history, written over 4000 years ago:

cuneiform tablet (L.2461)
from approximately 2000 BC
on display at the Istanbul Museum of
the Ancient Orient

The age-old practice of penning one's way to a woman's heart has stood the test of time as an introduction, an aphrodisiac, a powerful method of apology, a way to express oneself and even simply for entertainment. The general rule is that most people love a good writer, so it's only logical that women love to be wooed by a man who is good with words. But even if you're not a wordsmith, most women would prefer to have someone write them a not-so-perfect letter rather than no letter at all.

Your Goddess will no doubt appreciate your efforts to express yourself on paper for her. She will see it as you making an attempt to love her more, and that can only bring more cohesion, love, laughter and romance to your partnership. If that is your goal, then write her letters, write her love notes and even write short, sweet notes on her bathroom mirror. Tuck a note in her purse when she's not watching. Leave one in the coffee maker if that's the first thing she touches in the morning. The worst that can happen is she starts her day with a smile and considers it as a token of your love and affection for her.

They say the pen is mightier than the sword. This is actually one situation where that axiom holds true and you would do well to apply it as often as possible. If you're not that creative and don't know where to start or run out of things to say, get to the nearest search engine and type in "How do I write a love note?" Just do it. Do it now.

CHAPTER 23: TAKE CANDLELIT BATHS WITH HER

It can't be overstated how therapeutic, soothing, healing, sexy, relaxing and inspiring a nice, long, hot bath can be. I would go so far as to say especially to a woman. I would go even farther to say especially to a woman who has had a long day and wants to decompress.

What most women probably don't experience as much as they might like is to enjoy a nice intimate bath with their beloved. This is an area that I can personally assure you will benefit your love life and the cohesion in your relationship. The picture you see below is from a recent bath my beloved and I enjoyed during the last full moon. It was an amazing experience full of relaxation, connection, intimacy, love and magic.

If you aren't experienced with this kind of thing, don't fret. You're in luck! You are fortunate enough to live in the age of information where the internet can be searched successfully for anything imaginable. This includes, but is not limited to "how do I prepare a romantic bath" or "ideas for romantic baths for couples". Typing either of the previous two statements into a search engine should set you on a path of discovery that can quickly qualify you as a bath expert, leaving your Goddess doing two things. She will be wondering when/how you became such a romantic bath expert and she will know that you are attempting to love her more. Loving her more is the key.

Attempting goes a long way in love. Trust me. Just do it. Do it now.

CHAPTER 24: TURN OFF YOUR CELL PHONE

One of the biggest complaints from women about men throughout history is that men either choose not to or don't know how to do one thing...LISTEN.

As discussed in Chapter 7, learning to listen, hearing what is being listened to, and then considering what has been heard is paramount for healthy communication in a relationship. One of the biggest hindrances to the success of that process is the phone, specifically the cell phone.

We all have a cell phone, most of us have very intelligent smart phones and by now we have all been thoroughly indoctrinated in the roles they play in boredom relief. The trouble with cell phones is that most people have zero innerstanding of the chemistry involved in our addiction to these little devices and how that addiction is intricately woven into the infinite number of apps available for download on them.

According to an article at WebMD.com, "**Dopamine** is a type of neurotransmitter. Your body makes it, and your nervous system uses it to send messages between your brain and nerve cells. That's why it's sometimes called a chemical messenger. Dopamine plays a role in how we feel pleasure. It's a big part of our unique human ability to think and plan."

App and game developers are very aware of dopamine's role in our pleasure centers and have taken full advantage of this science by considering its effects and applying that knowledge to the development of their platforms, apps and software. Most end-users aren't aware of the chemical stimulation occurring inside of their brains as they are getting an instant, ever-so-brief "high" from someone liking their social media posts or from their latest one up against an opponent they're obliterating in the latest fad game.

Most people don't study science beyond high school, especially not chemistry, so most people will never truly innerstand what cell phones are doing to them and what exactly is the nature of their addiction to these little devices. I would advise any God who desires to love his Goddess more to go to a search engine and type in "dopamine and cell phones". This is not a request. This is a command. GO DO IT RIGHT THIS MINUTE!

It's not that difficult to innerstand how impeding a cell phone can be to basic communication within a relationship. That's why you must develop the habit of muting or turning off your cell phone when spending time that you are supposed to be dedicating wholly to your Goddess. I can't stress enough how much more loved that could make a Goddess feel. It screams to her that you're shutting out the world in favor of time alone with her and that is one of the most powerful ways you can show her that you desire to love her more. Trust me, just do it. Do it now.

CHAPTER 25: TAKE HER ON PICNICS AND CAMPING

Nature and romance go hand in hand for many reasons. Solitude, free from distraction is the most important thing that comes to mind, but aesthetic and connection are both close runners-up. There is nothing that can benefit a relationship in such a profound way as being alone in a beautiful, natural setting.

Camping is always a great way to escape the rigmarole of the daily grind and get connected to the true self without all the distractions of life bombarding your psyche. Add a little romance to that setting and voila! You've got a woman who can actually FEEL you loving her more. You won't have anything distracting you from giving her all your attention and that is one of the best ways to make your woman feel like a Goddess who is being loved more.

When camping is impossible, the next best thing is a picnic in the park or even in a nearby woods. The point is beautiful, natural scenery, solitude, quiet, good food and your beloved. This kind of opportunity to connect and effectively nourish your bond should be seized upon as often as possible, so do all that you can to squeeze picnics and camping into your love life.

Another benefit of the solitude of camping is that it provides a good deal of privacy that can be used to explore ritual and the use of ritual to broaden, energize, restore and/or heal aspects of your relationship. There are many ways to incorporate ritual into a relationship and I will be exploring some ideas on this later, but for now just remember that camping is a great space to implement your own rituals together. That can only make a relationship stronger and would also make any Goddess know instantly that she is being loved more. Just do it and let the magic begin!

CHAPTER 26: BREAK THE HABIT OF EYE WANDERING

Imagine that you spent longer than usual picking out the perfect outfit, cologne, jewelry, restaurant and all the trappings for a special date with your beloved. As you are enjoying dinner you can't help but notice that every attractive man that walks by your table catches the flirting eye of your partner. What do you think is going on in her head? Do you wonder what she might be fantasizing about as she's sizing up these other men, after you've invested so much of your time, energy and effort into attracting her focus tonight? How would that make you feel? Would you consider it offensive? Insulting? Rude? Inconsiderate? Selfish? Sleazy?

Wandering eyes are one of the most obvious ways your Goddess can tell that you haven't completely surrendered to her (and vice versa). When a person is so consumed with love and affection for their significant other and a sacred bond of divine love has become established, there is no desire to entertain another's affections because at this point all others' affections would be seen as a threat to the marvelously, holy and divine connection you already have.

When a divine connection of love and commitment has been consciously chosen, there is no desire for another because the complete magnificence of such a connection trumps any lesser carnal desires and lower vibrational sentiments. It's really that cut and dry. The magic created by this level of connection blows away childish games and foolish narratives for something so real only a fool would dare think to undermine it with vice of any sort.

It is innerstood that men who have spent a lifetime with their eyes wandering may experience difficulty ceasing that practice, but if one simply spends some meditation time imagining the first paragraph of this chapter over and over a few times, the reprogramming will begin and old habits will die as new relationship-guarding habits are formed to protect your bond and offer safety and security to your Goddess AND YOU, instead of having her wonder about your mind state.

Offering safety and security to your Goddess, lifts her up onto a pedestal of your surrender and reassures her that you are definitely loving her more. That is sure not to go unrewarded. Just do it.

CHAPTER 27: BE 100% AUTHENTIC IN EVERYTHING YOU THINK, DO AND SAY

The title of this chapter really should go without saying, but so should some other things I've felt compelled to write about in this book. After observing too many men who seem to need to be reminded of this, I find it absolutely paramount to admonish you to **BE 100% AUTHENTIC IN EVERYTHING YOU THINK, DO AND SAY!**

This means be authentic in everything you say and do to everyone, everywhere, every time, in every circumstance, for every reason, in every way and with every breath you take. If you don't operate with authenticity then how can you expect your Goddess or anyone else to?

You attract reflections of yourself in everyone you experience, so if you want authentic connections with authentic people then, my friend, you are going to have to operate with the utmost in unmovable, unshakable, unbuyable, unbreakable, irrevocably undeniable authenticity. A man whose moral compass moves for anything is a man who is not authentic.

It is quite difficult to maintain a mask when one's inner being isn't being reflected accurately. There are people who have learned to "act" very convincingly, for years even, however, sooner or later the charade must come to an end and the truth comes to light. When that happens, your integrity is shown to be in question and for many, if not most, people it's impossible to gain complete trust again. There will always be that question in the back of someone's mind, wondering if you're being untrustworthy again.

Needless to say, it's extremely important to be a man of your word, to be authentic in all you do, and let unquestionable integrity be the rule, not the exception, and this is especially true in the case of relationships. When dealing with a life partner, you're surrendering your all to someone and expecting them to do the same for the betterment of both parties involved. How can you expect authenticity unless you're offering the same?

If you're not prepared to be authentic then it's best to not enter into a lifelong partnership to begin with as you will only end up scarring yourself and your partner which creates a bigger problem than being lonely in the first place. Work on being authentic and make sure you are before you demand it from another. Just do it.

CHAPTER 28: SURRENDER TO HER

Once you have chosen the perfect Goddess for you, you are absolutely certain that beyond a shadow of a doubt you are putting the key in the lock and it's turning with ease, opening the perfect love for you and your partner, you are now ready to move toward complete surrender to each other.

Some hear the term "surrender" and don't see it as something to look forward to as the word can have connotations of loss, defeat and vulnerability, depending on how it's being used. My use of the term here, however, is completely the opposite of the most common interpretations of it. There is a huge difference between submission and surrender. The latter is willful. The prior is usually against one's will. Choice is a very powerful indicator that you haven't lost your power or will.

When I say surrender to your partner, I don't mean bow down and lose the game. I mean lift your partner up and empower your partner to do the same to you. When two powerful people surrender to each other completely, neither has to be made less powerful. When full surrender is given with pure intention and completely in the spirit of love and truth, then it can only bring strength to everyone involved and, most important of all, to the relationship. Surrender is, in all actuality, the foundation of any true lifelong partnership.

CHAPTER 29: MAKE GODLY LOVE TO HER

If you have to ask your Goddess if you "made her cum', then you didn't. It's really that simple.

Not the most sacred place to begin a chapter about loving your Goddess more divinely, but for some men, it's necessary to begin there. Allow me to explain.

Many, if not most, of us receive programming that gears us toward pacification of carnal desires that are grounded in the lower chakras (or energy centers). The lowest is our root chakra which is all about survival (stability, security and our most basic needs). For many of us, this includes sex, and as much of it as we can get.

As men, we have historically abused sex in many ways to satiate our desires and much of that has been at the expense of women's dignity, satisfaction and needs. This has not always been the case, of course, but it has occurred enough to warrant this discussion.

The abuse men have subjected women to for millennia has given rise to much generational karma as well as trauma that has been handed down from mother to daughter for more generations than we can count. The healing process for this and also present-life trauma can be a slow, painful process for many women. One thing that has become very apparent to me throughout my experience is that healing that trauma can occur exponentially faster when a man takes part in the process and provides a space of safety, innerstanding and love to a healing woman.

Holding space for your Goddess to move through trauma,

remember her divinity and reclaim her power is the most life-changing way to love her more. There are many elements to this process and it can be a difficult road, especially if you are personally responsible for any of the wounding, but the benefits of healing past traumas will give your relationship a miraculous makeover.

Men have experienced much trauma throughout history as well, so healing your own wounds must also be a part of this process. The strongest couples are the ones who have found a way to make it through the healing process together, holding space for each other and being the innerstanding shoulder the other needs to feel safe while moving through the shadow work that must be done.

There are many online resources, psychological medical professionals, shamans, counselors and more that can be sought out to assist in healing the specific traumas you both may seek to heal, and that would be another book entirely on its own, so I'll leave it up to you to do some research on that process and assist your Goddess with moving through it.

Once that process is in motion, it will become apparent at some point, if you don't already know, that women love orgasms just as much, if not more, than men. But here's the kicker: nature designed a woman's orgasm to TRIGGER yours! This means that if making love is performed with love, care, unselfish consideration and eye-gazing connection, she will almost ALWAYS reach climax before you. This will trigger your own release and bring you both soul-serving, tantric, deep-rooted satisfaction that won't leave your Goddess (or you) feeling used, dirty (not spiritually, at least lol), cheap, unloved, unwanted, unsexy, misunderstood, hurt, unappreciated or any of those nasty mental dispositions that none of us wants to feel.

The fact is that when a divine connection is had in a relationship, the sex becomes better than it could ever be otherwise. I can personally attest to this from my own experience and admonish you to explore this with your Goddess. There's an old saying that I just made up..."Once you go divine, you'll never rewind!" Get a tattoo of it if you have to, but whatever you do, DON'T FORGET IT!

Every woman longs to belong to a man that she can safely surrender to, be treated like a Goddess by, be satisfied by in every way and someone who will at least match her in doing the work. When a woman finds THAT man, there is no limit to what she would do to please him, keep him safe, make him feel loved and generally take care of him. This is what relationships are supposed to be about. A "LOVE" love is supposed to blow the minds of both parties and, despite the popular yet erroneous assumption that the spark must fade, last a lifetime and beyond. If that's not what you're looking to do then why not save someone (and yourself) some heartache and simply remain single. Anything less would be a lie.

Once godly, divine, sacred, tantric lovemaking is coming into play, it is mandatory that massage become a regular integral part of it all. There are many ways to make love that genitals don't always have to be a part of. I would personally suggest that massage be adopted as part of, and aside from, lovemaking, but either way, the benefits to a relationship that massage can bring are amazing and should not be overlooked. You are one massage away from a good mood!

Massage lowers production of the stress hormone, cortisol, while increasing dopamine, serotonin and endorphins (all the feel good stuff!). It also slows down heartbeat rates by about 10 beats per minute. Massaging your Goddess will cause the oxytocin levels in her brain to rise, and in case you didn't know, oxytocin is one of the chemicals that drive attachment! The benefits are probably endless, but I'm sure you get the picture. Massage is not just a luxury. It's a way to a healthier, happier life and relationship.

I can write an entire book on massage, also, but there are so many wonderful books on the subject already, that I would recommend grabbing one or two and experimenting together as a couple to find what you both enjoy and what works best for you.

There is one massage-related thing I must recommend, though, from personal experience that is going to change your love life forever if you're not already aware of it: COCONUT OIL!!! The benefits coconut oil can add to a relationship, especially in the bedroom are only as finite as your imaginations are.

I've discovered coconut oil to be the best personal lubriCOULD money can buy. It will literally make you stop buying lubriCAN'Ts and start buying something with many more uses than simply in the bedroom. I've personally been using coconut oil as a substitute for skin lotion for about 15 years and I consistently get compliments about how youthful and vibrant my skin looks. Trust me when I say that no human being over 40 years old will ever get tired of hearing that!

I recommend that couples who bathe together take turns massaging coconut oil into each other's epidermis layer after each shower. It's healthier for your skin and can be integrated into a daily ritual of sensual touching that is bound to keep the spark alive and enhance your attraction to each other. That brings me to another important point that I'd like to make regarding lovemaking away from the bed...RITUAL. We will discuss this more in the final chapter.

Put a daily massage reminder in your calendar. Set aside quiet time away from the kids, electronics and other distractions so that you can provide (and receive) some stress-free, quality time dedicated solely to massaging your Goddess and making her feel loved more. It's almost impossible to go wrong on this one, so master the art of healing and sensual massage and your relationship will benefit greatly. That is a promise and a guarantee or your money back.

Massage is life. Just do it. Do it now. And don't ever stop.

CHAPTER 30: MANIFEST TOGETHER

If you've made it this far in this book, your mind should already be exploring ways that implementing the ideas, concepts, methods and protocols contained herein will bring magic to your relationship. If not, then begin the implementation process of these ideas and as you do more and more of that, more magic will begin to appear.

Aside from the magic that will naturally appear as you incorporate these ideas into your connection, there is plenty of magic to be explored in the combining of your manifestation capabilities. Every human is a creator, made in the image and likeness of the most divine Creator who bestowed on each of us the power to manifest our will and intention into being via the use of frequency.

Here's a brief frequency lesson:
All is ATUM.
ATUM=atom=Adam, thus anATOMy.
Your anatomy is the macrocosm of an atom or an ATUM or "THE" ATUM.
Your anatomy is the microcosm of the solar system.
All is ATUM means that all is frequency.
All frequency is sound.
All is sound.
Sound and light are waves of the same energy so sound=light so All is light
ALL meaning everything, including you, your Goddess, your thoughts and her thoughts
Everything begins as thought
Thought=all=the ALL

All is thought.
You produce thought by thinking
You produce all=You produce the ALL
You are a thought "factory" and produce this entire universe every second of every minute of every day, forever and ever.
You always have.
You always will.
Your thought and the emotions that affect it is your power. Gaining control over your thought processes and your emotions IS YOUR POWER.

After studying the Bible and holy scriptures from every religion and culture on the planet for almost 40 years (yes, since I started reading at age 3 the Bible and commentary on it has been an integral part of my studies) I've come to interpret the whole of Jesus's teachings to mean that Jesus is in fact in each and every one of us whom he called Gods. He exists as what some call the Christ Consciousness and is the inherent divinity that is available to all worthy truth-seekers who embark on the alchemical journey some call the path of enlightenment.

In Matthew 18:20 (KJV), *Jesus stated that,* **"For where two or three are gathered together in my name, there am I in the midst of them."**

I interpret this scripture to mean that when two or more Gods or Goddesses, especially those who are in tune with the Christ Consciousness within, gather their focus (their thought and the emotions that affect those thoughts) on the same intention, then at that point the power of the Creator steps in to bring that intention to fruition with more speed and precision. At that point, the Universe begins to move faster and dedicate more ATUMic or atomic resources towards attracting the intended goal towards you.

None of that is speculation. All if that is in fact law. It's difficult to put some of it into English, but as a shaman who has traveled interdimensionally countless times I've come to learn a thing or two about love and life that it's difficult to grasp without going through the work necessary to have those experiences. I've done my best here to present what I've learned from those travels combined with my life experiences to help you and other men gain from my losses, lessons and victories.

If you haven't already, I suggest you and your Goddess build a love altar together or do some research into building one if you don't know how. Buy a "Jericho Rose" and water it together as a ritual to bless your love. Research other love rituals that you can use as a starting point for creating rituals of your own that you, as a couple, perform together. This suggestion could turn into another book entirely, so you'll have to do some research on ways for a couple to use a love altar and perform rituals together, but trust that this is the direction you want to head in with your Goddess.

I suggest you and your Goddess do some research into alchemy. I'd suggest books like The Hermetica (start with the Emerald Tablets of Thoth, if you feel you're ready) and other books that give instruction to those seeking spiritual enlightenment. The more ancient the book is, the better. You will no doubt discover ways to ritualize your love and your lives and that can only bring you closer and show both of you that the other desires to love you more.

CONCLUSION:

For as long as it is possible I will be available in life to offer mentorship, guidance and ideas on loving and lighting the way, so feel free to post questions on the social media pages for this book or publisher and I'll respond to all that I am able to. I am also available for personal consultation which you can access by using the author contact information provided.

I wish you and your Goddess love, blessings and good fortune on your journey to learning to love her more and I pray that you let the world know how you have benefited from this book by leaving a review where you purchased it from. Then pass it along to a man (or woman) who needs to read it. Thank you and much love.

ABOUT THE AUTHOR

Christopher Conrad Tolen

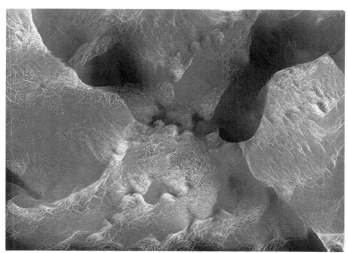

Christopher Conrad Tolen was born and raised in South Carolina to a family who advocated reading. An early bloomer who started reading and writing at age 3, Tolen grew up with access to his mother's scientific and esoteric library, and spent much of his youth with his nose in books that some might have called out of his league.

At age 21 he moved to Chicago where he spent 22 years before moving to central Florida where he currently works as a healer, freelance photographer and author.

When he's not writing or gardening he enjoys reading, traveling, yoga, biking, Scrabble, chess and spending time with his beloved, family and friends.

If you enjoyed any of his works, please leave a review, then tag and follow @tolenmedia to be
informed when the next book is released and also for details on merchandise and the latest news.

Your contribution for this work is allowing Tolen to devote precious time and resources to his next creative endeavor. The world can always use more inspiration and smiles.

He can be found online at http://www.tolen.media or on FB and IG at @tolenmedia.

BOOKS BY THIS AUTHOR

Quotos®: Inspirational Quotes
With Photos To Match

See life vividly through the eyes of a shaman who has learned to live each day full of optimistic belief and appreciation for owning one's limitless potential.Born in the 70's, actor, author, singer, father and photographer Christopher Conrad Tolen reflects on what is possible as he travels the globe sharing and learning insights and continuing on his personal journey of self-discovery after a not-so-smooth road to manhood."QUOTOS" is the first in a series and features almost 50 sensational original photographs matched with inspirational insights from some of history's brightest minds. You will find in this book the essence of a man self-realized, words and thoughts that he used to transform himself and live by and that you are sure to enrich your own life with. Let this book remind you of the endless possibilities of nature in all her majesty, and where you might grab a perfect gift of inspiration to give away to others.At an age when many are beginning to slow down, Conrad is ready for the next adventure, always creating, always inspiring and being inspired. He admonishes us all to choose love, live joyfully and appreciate the little things.

And I Color: An Adult Coloring Book For
Stress Relief And Inspiration

Get out your rainbow colors and make today beautiful! Here's another book in the Color My Visions® Series delivers more breathtaking mandalas for coloring your stress away, all completely original creations of artist/photographer Christopher Conrad. Soothing inspiration is yours as you breathe colorful life into some of the most intricate symmetry put into mandala form, each accompanied by a thoughtful, colorful quote about the very subject of COLOR! Perfect for any age, each ready-to-color page is mystical, magical and hypnotic. The perfect gift for yourself or a loved one. Providing hours of mesmerizing fun while discovering India's most ancient symbols of color and sound. Release your mind with 60 pages of coloring fun!

The Awesome And Amazing Adventures Of Spoodow

Go on an adventure with the world's latest and greatest character in a new kinda comic book that will delight readers of all ages. Rated G for all audiences, this light-hearted tome of silliness will generate laughs for anyone who picks it up as they fall in love with Spoodow and his attempts to get through life while giving as many scary scares as possible to anyone he can. Avoiding the amazingly boring Boredow Beast is what he does best because keeping the boredom away is Spoodow's number one goal! His antics and wisecracks are funny, witty and good humor for the whole family. Make sure to follow @Spoodow on Instagram and Facebook to keep up with more adventures in the future."Let's go on and ADVENTURE!!!"

Made in the USA
Columbia, SC
18 April 2024

34298741R00050